THE MAKING OF WEALTH

PRINCIPLES FOR WEALTH CREATION

S.O. KEHINDE (SOK)

Ordering Information:

Books to Life Marketing Ltd
128 City Road, London, EC1V 2NX, UK

Printed in the United States of America

CONTENTS

THE CREATIVE POWER OF MAN

GETTING RICH IS a result of doing things in a certain way. That is, there are principles to follow. Opportunities are not monopolized. No one builds a fence around wealth to exclude others from acquiring it. There are an abundance of opportunities for the man who will swim with the tide rather than go against it. Wealth is an acronym. The full expression of Wealth is "What everyone aspires lovingly to have".

Part of a successful life is to aspire to be healthy and wealthy. Health comes before wealth, the reason why we always say "health is wealth".

There are the four sensible and sensitive questions of life which need to be answered by an individual intending to succeed in any life endeavor

(i)   Where Am I coming from?
(ii)   Why Am I here?
(iii) Where Am I going?
(iv)   How do I get there?

The questions above are of utmost importance that every purposeful man must be able to ask himself and answer. These questions help every individual to determine how to fulfill his destiny and achieve maximum success.

While God is identified with creative power, the fact that He created man in His image bestows man the same power to create and we witness this in the various developments all over the world. Human beings' superior mental capacity makes them to be in a better position to use their creative power to add value to themselves, the significant others, and their society at large.

The Psalmist extols the creative wisdom of the Almighty God when he said "How many are your works, LORD! In wisdom you made them all. The earth is full of your creatures (Psalm 104:24). So man has the power to create anything, within the limitation of God.

There is however the need for man to have Advancing Mind in whatever he does, it is the human mind that drives one to success or failure in what one is doing, with faith and purpose that better things lie ahead. It must be understood that in the scientific method of doing things, we encounter the competitive plane and the creative plane on our way to progress. The more men who become wealthy on the competitive plane, the worse for others; the more who get richer on the creative plane the better for others. We can conclude that progress is achieved when the world experiences a situation whereby more get rich on the creative plane. God was not competitive but creative and liberally supplied all human needs.

Human economic solutions can only be achieved when a greater number of people practice the scientific method of creativity and become wealthy in the process. The multiplier effect of these results is the wealth of a nation. However, an individual must have the determination to become wealthy and direct action toward the realization. Not only must your thoughts and actions be focused on the determination, you must believe you can achieve wealth and struggle toward achieving it.

Simply put - Readiness + Determination + Thoughts + Belief + Actions bring about Result. The Result in this respect is Wealth. You can see here that your mind, body and soul are all involved. The Concept of Wealth comes from the mind. Whatever you determine must first be conceived, before taking steps to bring it to reality. The PBR formula is relevant here - you pray, believe and receive. John Mason is of the opinion that you may succeed if nobody else believes in you but you cannot succeed if you do not believe in yourself. Your mindset plays an important and active role in your achievements, financial or otherwise. In other words your achievements spring up from ideas, because ideas rule the world. Ideology which is a system of ideas and ideals that form the basis of economic, social and political theory and policy, offer principles for social and political development and shape the direction of a nation. This is because the normative beliefs and values that an individual or group hold are the product of their behaviors and actions. In other words, you are what you behold. You get what you have affection for. Certain important things to do include::

(I) GRAB THE OPPORTUNITY

Opportunity may appear in different forms. It may come as a direct and positive fortune that gladdens the heart or be disguised in the form of misfortune or temporary defeat. The fact that not all opportunities come in the form of fortune makes it difficult at times to recognise an event as opportunity, especially when it comes as a misfortune. The statement 'every disappointment is a blessing' is in support of this view.

To some people the fear of failure may make it difficult for them to recognise opportunity when it comes their way and that is the reason why determination at achieving a desired end is important. Your desire for success in all endeavors must be greater than your fear of failure before you can achieve success. It is also a senseless waste of time and energy to seek opportunity without a purpose or aim in life i.e. expression of the goal toward which the opportunity will be directed. This is the reason for one to engage in Positive Thinking and behave rationally. Set an aim in life; you can keep changing your goals as you meet them. A goal-oriented person has an attractive personality.

Rational behavior gives you the sense of maintaining a pleasing life-style that will endear you to a large number of people who can assist you to fulfil your destiny. Remember that you can build a beautiful place in life, but you need people to bring your dream to reality. You must therefore develop the ability to adjust with others and understand the way different people perceive the world. This makes communication effective and gives you the opportunity to receive the much needed information and ideas to launch your efforts into success.

(II) BELIEF IN YOURSELF

To be yourself in a world that is constantly trying to make you something else is the greatest accomplishment (Ralph Waldo Emerson). Be confident of your personality and identify your potential. Direct it toward achieving the purpose for which you are here on earth. Myles Munroe says "When purpose is not clear, abuse is inevitable". Do not abuse your purpose. Be wise as a person rather than being clever. Know that you are born for a purpose here on the earth planet and you must fulfill that purpose, for maximum life achievement. You need to get wisdom and understanding to identify your purpose. You are not born by accident, there is a reason for your existence. That reason must be clearly understood by every individual. Let us wait a minute and think on the subject matter of 'Purpose'. Purpose in life must be identified as its discovery is a roadmap to every other thing. Before your wealth, you must be able to determine how you intend to utilize it for maximum fulfillment. Since wealth without direction is purposeless, the first problem to solve before aspiring for it is to answer the question, 'for what purpose'?

(III) POSITIVE METHODOLOGY

Methodology is a system of methods used in a particular area of activity. It is simply the systematic, theoretical analysis of the methods of knowledge that deals with the creation and use of technical means in the performance of our various duties. Technology therefore signifies an advancement in methodology. Wealth creation is tied to the use of technology and having a correct knowledge of the operations and practical demonstration of the various skills in use. In practically all spheres of life endeavors, the conventional ways of doing things have given room to the modern technique. We need not say that what makes the modern world achieve rapid development is the use of technology. No one wanting to reap the harvest of this development can be ignorant of the modern technique. Growth and development are governed by principles. Positive Methodology is therefore part of the principles for wealth creation.

Whatever the methodology or approach used in any life endeavor to accomplish the goal, there are three key attributes to achieve success. They are:

(A) *Aptitude*

It is simply a natural ability to do something. It is a component of a competence to do a certain kind of work in a certain way, at a certain level with maximum achievement. Since it is a skill, aptitude can be learned. No one in any profession can demonstrate his/her competence above his/her aptitude. Aptitude therefore determines competence for achievement. But since it can be learnt, you can improve on it.

(B) *Attitude*

Attitude connotes a settled way of thinking or feeling about something. The manifestation of attitude is human behavior or character. If you have a truculent or uncooperative attitude toward something, you can not excel in that thing. For instance if a teacher has a biassed mind for a course, he or she can not be an effective teacher of that course. Psychologically, attitude is a construct, a mental and emotional entity that inheres in or characterizes an object. Your attitude or opinion, positive or negative matters in the demonstration of your skill to perform a task. Our attitude can either attract people to us, or hurt and drive people away from us. This must be changed if it inhibits progress and advancement.

(C) *Passion*

Passion has to do with your emotion. It is a powerful feeling of your love for something. If a professional doctor, engineer, teacher or practitioner of any other discipline will succeed, it suggests he must demonstrate interest and love for the discipline to achieve a feat. It is your passion that will drive your interest to search for the appropriate methodology to perform effectively or to improve your skill. Contributions to progress by the individuals depend on these attributes combined, their aptitude, attitude and passion.

Man as a God being, fearfully and wonderfully made, was divinely designed by God and destined to succeed and be wealthy, through his creative mind. He was also discerned to unravel the hidden riches of the secret places. This truth can be supported by the massive exploratory power given to exploit the pervasive material and mineral resources used for developmental purposes. There is no doubt that man is second to God in wisdom. To belittle or abuse this opportunity by man's inaction in any way is an aberration.

Only the blessed ones can be a source of blessing to others and the purpose God created humans in His image is to serve as a blessing to the world. Wealth creation is worthy of all acceptance and must be pursued passionately and with great obsession.

(IV) WISDOM

It is important to apply wisdom to our effort to acquire wealth. Wisdom is a concept that embraces prudence, knowledge and discretion. It is a principle of understanding the right thing to do and the appropriate time to do it. "Wisdom has built her house; she has hewn her seven pillars" Proverbs 9:1). A man of wisdom is a man who understands how to apply knowledge constructively. He takes counsel and puts the gains to diligent use. He walks in the way of righteousness and pursues his course with an honest mind. He is hardworking and a man of integrity. "The wise of heart will receive commandments, but a babbling fool will come to ruin. Whoever walks in integrity walks securely, but he who makes his way crooked will be found out" (Proverbs 10:8–9).

(V) SUCCESS AND POSITIVE MINDSET

We will discuss this topic with reference to acquisition of knowledge and understanding through *thought, experience* and *the senses* i.e. Human Cognition. Cognition refers, quite simply, to thinking. There are the obvious applications of conscious reasoning/doing. Cognition includes different processes, like learning, attention, memory, language, reasoning, decision making etc. which form part of our intellectual development and experience. This suggests that in actual fact, cognition is the working of the mind, the thinking faculty. To be a success and fulfil maximum attainment, our cognition must not be faulty. For success to come to reality, we must have a positive mindset and believe in like manner, since cognitive behavior can either be positive or negative.

What is Mindset? Mindset is simply a set of assumptions, methods or notations held by someone or a group. In politics we talk of collective mindsets that emanate from the thinking or desire of the leaders in politics. It is either positive or negative, progressive or retrogressive, forward looking, backward looking or fixed. Mindset is actually the level of a man's desire for something and it is the starting point of all achievements. It plays a major role in self motivation and achievements - Need for achievement, and has been the reason for many successes and failures depending on the nature of mindset, whether positive or negative. Positive mindset is progressive and desired for achievement and growth.

A man with a positive mindset never admits temporary defeats or perhaps permits some failures as the end of a matter. Failure is a trickster with a keen sense of irony and cunning at the point when success or achievement of a course is almost within reach. Be persistent and try to prove that "no" does not necessarily mean the actual "no" but "next opportunity". It takes a persistent person to know that whatever is conceived and believed by the mind can be achieved. Also, with determination to achieve, you can create value, project value and market value which suggests that one can turn his/her potential and talents to products that can be sold to create wealth.

The desire for wealth is born out of determination and obsession to achieve a great purpose in life through the use of ideas, new ways of doing things, new leaders, new inventions, new methodology etc. The working principles of the human mind must be applied to the fullest in the attainment of any goal. In the same way, accumulation of wealth cannot be left to chance, good fortune and luck, but to a lot more dreaming, hoping, wishing, desiring and planning. You must desire and believe that you can acquire wealth and take a pragmatic action toward fulfilling that purpose. No one wants poverty which is an infectious disease that can only be cured with wealth. Wealth, on the other hand can only be acquired through a strong determination and positive mindset.

Learn from the successes of the past heroes of achievements who have made use of opportunities and have achieved great heights and made every convenience that makes life more pleasant for us today. Great people of the old who were originators of civilization of today were dreamers whose determined efforts at achieving the dreams have launched into progress in this changed world. Big businesses of the present day and investments were the thinking of old men and women of the past. But their legacies left behind are the enjoyment of the present world. From generation to generation this will be the order of events.

It is important that to move forward, we must catch the spirit of the great pioneers of the past, whose dreams have given value to the civilization we enjoy presently. Their determination and persistence saw their dreams come true. They did not succumb to temporary defeat or failure, knowing too well that every failure brings with it the seed of an equivalent success. In actual fact, they regarded every mistake as a learning process. Persistence and perseverance make the dreams come to physical reality. Dreams are not born out of indifference, laziness or lack of ambition; yet, every practical dreamer does not quit but pursues with vigor and ambition the realization of the dream, and through heartbreaking struggles.

CHAPTER 1

FAITH IN GOD

THE BOOK OF Hebrews defines faith as "confidence in what we hope for and assurance about what we do not see" (11:1). Psalms 146:3–4 says "Do not put your trust in princes, in human beings, who cannot save. When their spirit departs, they return to the ground; on that very day their plans come to nothing". "God is the maker of heaven and earth, the sea and everything in them - he remains faithful forever"(6). In all circumstances the providential nature of God demands that all our needs are provided by him alone. He created all living and nonliving things without exception and provided for all his creations according to their needs. It stands to reason therefore that we must trust in him for everything and work according to his guiding principles to be able to reap the harvest of our labor, because God "provides food for the cattle and for the young ravens. He strengthens the bars of your gates and blesses your people within you. He grants peace to your borders and satisfies you with the finest of wheat" (Psalm 147:9, 13–14).

It is instructive to note that anyone seeking reputation, recognition and wealth needs God's wisdom and power of discernment because riches and wealth are hidden treasures. It takes a man of wisdom and insight to locate them. They are not got on a platter of gold but God gives to people who fear him and work according to his principles. Not only that, it pleases God to enable people to enjoy the fruit of their toils (Ecclesiastes 2:21–26).

"The earth is the LORD's and everything in it, the world and all who live in it" (Psalm 24:1). Since everything belongs to him, nothing in the world can be appropriated without his consent. "Do not be wise in your own eyes, fear the LORD and shun evil. This will bring health to your body and nourishment to your bones. Honor the LORD with your wealth, with the firstfruits of all your crops, then your barns will be filled to overflowing and your vats will brim over with new wine" (Proverbs 3:9–10).

The Psalmist is more elaborate when he declares "Praise him you highest heavens and you waters above the skies. Let them praise the name of the LORD for at his command they were created, and he established them forever and ever - he issued a decree that will never pass away. Praise the LORD from the earth, you great seas creatures and all ocean depths, lightning and hail, snow and clouds, stormy winds that do his bidding, you mountains and all hills, fruit trees and all cedars, wild animals and all cattle, small creatures and flying birds, kings of the earth and all nations, you princes and all rulers on earth, young men and women, old men and children. Let them praise the name of the LORD, for his name alone is exalted, his splendor is above the earth and the heavens" (148:4–13). And he closed the songs "Let everything that has breath praise the LORD. Praise the LORD" (150:6).

From all accounts God is the owner of the universe and everything therein, be it human, natural and material resources and he directs the process by which they are utilized through human beings. Every material blessing belongs to him and all human efforts to acquire wealth without him are made in futility (Psalm 127:1–2).

The reason for which we live is to satisfy our soul. Spirit or mind and body. The command by God for human beings to multiply is meant to be fulfilled in every direction of life. Multiplication is multi-dimensional. Poverty is therefore alien to the components of man - mind, soul and body and happened to him by not doing things in the Certain Way which has been provided. However I do not want to be unduly scientific by not recognizing the fact that God provided the way to riches, honor, wealth and recognition, so that humans would not boast of acquiring anything by their own strength but that it pleased him to make us prosper and increase in all areas of endeavor. The fulfillment for God's promise of prosperity is obedience and this signifies having faith in him who has promised. Anything short of this belief in God's providence would sound agnostic or atheistic, and this is not the intention of this writer

However, we believe there are certain things God wouldn't do to make us wealthy if we fail to do our part of the bid. There are consequences for not fulfilling the motive for which we live. Our purpose in life. For instance if we live for the body alone depriving the existence of the mind and soul, or we live either for soul or mind depriving the existence of the body. It is loathsome to deny any of the three and we see that real life means the complete expression of all that man can give forth through body, mind and soul. No man can be happy unless the trio of body, soul and mind are fully expressed and exerted. Each of them has functions to perform to make man a whole and thoroughly bred being. God is also happy when man is aware of this fact. Inaction of any of the three - the body, mind and soul is an abomination to God. The result is unexpressed possibility, or function not performed which finds expression in unsatisfied desire. Desire is possibility seeking expression or function seeking performance.

Physically, man requires certain basic utilities for the body to live fully. Good food, comfortable clothing, good housing with ventilation for good health, freedom and rest. Without these, the body becomes inertia, and God will not provide all these without human effort. Man cannot live fully in mind without exertion of the brain by reading books and devotion to study them, opportunity for travel and observation, or without intellectual companionship. Full mind is developed through intellectual recreations, objects and works of art and beauty for him to behold and appreciate. To live fully- developed in the soul, man must have love, expression of which is appreciated when we give out. Love is denied expression by poverty, since you do not give out what you do not have. The soul is fully expressed and happy when we are merciful and show love to all people. The consciousness of loving and being loved brings a warmth and richness to life that nothing else can bring (Oscar Wilde). Since love is expressed through our wealth, it must be at the back of every right-thinking person that your wealth is purposeless if your aim is to acquire it for self lust and pride (Matthew 19:21–22).

Our faith in God is anchored on obedience to him and living a virtuous life. We must be industrious and shun the common vices that hinder achievement of prosperity and wealth accumulation. We should not because we want to be wealthy, become corrupt and amass wealth wrongly. "Listen, my son, accept what I say, and the years of your life will be many. I instruct you in the way of wisdom and lead you along straight paths. When you walk, your steps will not be hampered; when you run, you will not stumble" (Proverbs 4:10–11). "Wealth is worthless on the day of wrath, but righteousness delivers from death" (Proverbs 11:4). "The blessing of the LORD brings wealth, without painful toil for it" (Proverbs 10:22). "Ill-gotten treasures have no lasting value, but righteousness delivers from death (Proverbs 10:2). "The fear of the LORD is the beginning of wisdom and knowledge of the Holy One is understanding. For through wisdom your days will be many and years will be added to your life" (Proverbs 9:10–11).

Faith is one of the most powerful of the major positive emotions. The other major positive emotions are love and sex. When the three are blended, they have the effect of working on thought in such a way that it reaches the subconscious mind, where it is changed into its spiritual equivalent that induces a response from infinite intelligence. Faith and Desire work together but the two emanate from the mind. We must recognise the existence of Faith and Desire before we can put them to action. We must also recognise the unlimited power of the mind to contain whatever we have faith to achieve. Be it riches or poverty, intellectual property, failure, successful attainment, financial freedom etc. It is our faith that will energize our desire to project it into reality. "So do not throw away your confidence, it will be richly rewarded. You need to persevere so that when you have done the will of God, you will receive what he has promised" (Hebrews 10:35–36). We must obey the mind as it communicates positive virtues and reject the vices. "But whoever looks intently into the perfect law that gives freedom and continues in it - not forgetting what they have heard but doing it - they will be blessed in what they do" (James 1:25). Trusting and having faith in God brings riches, honor and prosperity. One who loves God and does his will, through the effort directed by God will be wealthy. Rendering wealth to people is the liberal way God rewards hard work, honesty and integrity. "The LORD detests dishonest scales, but accurate weights find favor with him" (Proverbs 11:1). "The integrity of the upright guides them but the unfaithful are destroyed by their duplicity" (Proverbs 11:3) "The LORD detests those whose hearts are perverse, but he delights in those whose ways are blameless" (Proverbs 11:20).

Without wealth it will be impossible to serve God or please him. As a matter of fact, the purpose of God for humanity is for the individuals and nations to transform the world, a task that would be impossible if poverty is the order of the day. Evidence of this abounds all over the universe. The wealth of a nation determines its position in the comity of nations and the recognition enjoyed. What is required of the individual is to work hard in an honest way to amass wealth. However God bestows wealth. "I love those who love me, and those who seek me find me. With me are riches and honor, enduring wealth and prosperity. My fruit is better than fine gold, what I yield surpasses choice silver. I walk in the way of righteousness, along the paths of justice, bestowing a rich inheritance on those who love me and making their treasures full (Proverbs 8:17–21).

The conclusion of this chapter is clear. That God is providential. He created all human beings, animals, birds and plants. Provided material and mineral and natural resources beyond measure for their sustenance. It is not open to any controversy that every source of potential resources to fulfil God's purpose and reach maximum fulfillment can only come to us through him, and when we do not lose sight of his dominion over all creations. It is quite understandable also that God nurtured every creation to enjoy the fullness of life and that he will not create anything he can not nurture and provide for.

Any failure to recognise this fact and regard God as the source of life is a deliberate refusal to honor the source of all human existence. This can only result in failure. Peradventure through some hard work a level of success is achieved, this can not be enduring as it can only lead to pride which is the first step to destruction. It is also a deliberate refusal to retain God's knowledge in one's mind which may lead also to reprobation that God is the essence of our being. This is nothing but agnosticism, and the Bible confirms that an agnostic is a fool. Besides, wealth obtained through pride can not endure (Proverbs 8:13).

We must note and understand that everything depends on God's mercy and that righteousness is obtained by faith not by works. "Send me your light and your faithful care. Let them lead me, let them bring me to your holy mountain to the place where you dwell (Psalm 43:3). God knows the secrets of the heart (Psalm 44:22). Our faith in God is of utmost importance before we can receive his blessing. We must obtain the presence of God before we can receive his present. The irony is the fact that faith is an abstract, invisible thing and difficult to appraise. But, at least, an individual should be able to assess the level of his/her faith.

GOOD HEALTH

(1) INTRODUCTION

> "Dear friend, I pray that you may enjoy good health and that all may go well with you, just as you are progressing spiritually" (3rd John:2)

A WISE SAYING attests to the fact that "If wealth is lost nothing is lost, if health is lost, something is lost but if the character is lost, all is lost". This statement buttresses the importance of health. At least health is "something". Good health is the source of wealth thereby confirming the belief that "health is wealth" and our ability to sustain it is the first step to creating wealth. "Above all else, guard your heart, for everything you do flows from it" (Proverbs 4:23). Our heart is the spring-well of life and it is important to note that every right-thinking person must do everything possible to protect his heart from harm by taking actions that will prevent the heart from diseases, so as not to shorten his/her life span unnecessarily. Everything possible must be done to keep the heart free from worry, the reason why the word of God warns to always cast our anxiety off the mind but unto God. So you need to relax, refresh and relate well in order to stay healthy, awaiting your wealth to arrive. Do not look at the appearance of sickness, think healthy even when you are surrounded by diseases and do everything possible to free your environment from diseases. Aspire to live a healthy life-style, take a good diet, regular exercise and live in a well ventilated house, to enjoy the privilege of good health. We cannot live fully in mind, soul and body as a healthy person if our life-style, diet and actions contradict the rule of hygiene.

Good health is derived from getting ourselves rid of undesirable and excessive toil and surrounding ourselves with aesthetic beauty capable of increasing our well-being in body, mind and soul. Good health is determined by strict adherence to medical advice. Medical experts believe that to live a life of well-being requires some daily healthy lifestyles and habits that will prevent illness, ensure long life and prevent untimely death. According to medical experts, one major cause of fatal health issues like stroke, hypertension, heart diseases, diabetes and other life threatening diseases is troubled heart. This signifies that when the heart is troubled, your body will not be at peace. A healthy human being, whose heart is at peace will live to multiply life by being creative and productive. He will have the rest of mind to create value, project value and market value, which is a fundamental activity that improves the life of others. The conclusion is that only when one is healthy can one be positioned to follow the principles of prosperity and work smart to get rich and affect others positively.

Self discipline and control is a good thing for a healthy life. Man needs to suppress base desires and ensure restraint to live a healthy life. A drunk-ard, an adulterous person and someone who indulges himself in various health-challenging vices will be weak in mind, soul and body to live a healthy life and be a blessing to himself, Anything risky to one's life must be avoided to be able to affect other people's life positively, and create the much-needed wealth for self. A person who lives a careless life can not be the delight of God, since he will find it too difficult to render any useful service to God and humanity. He becomes a risk to himself and a source of vices and viruses to his significant others. Daniel in the Bible was a good example of a man who lived a disciplined life in Babylon. Joseph in Egypt was another self-controlled person. Both were able to master their lives and became a success in a strange land.

(II) SPIRITUAL HEALTH VERSUS PHYSICAL HEALTH

Let me start by reminding you about your nature. "So God created mankind in his own image, in the image of God he created them" (Genesis 1:27). In a man's life, both sensual and spiritual health are essential for earthly success. Manifolding blessings remain the portion of the prudent man that works in collaboration with perfect matured and healthy individuals. You must maintain a good habit to build a pleasing personality. Cleanliness, punctuality, sincerity help to positively change your personality. We must understand the fact that we are God being whom he created for his purposes and not to be sick or encounter diseases. "The Lord will keep you free from every disease. He will not inflict on you the horrible diseases you knew in Egypt but he will inflict them on all who hate you" (Deuteronomy 7:15). "No one living in Zion will say I am ill" (Isaiah 33:24a). This simply portrays the fact that God is always interested in our health and will keep us safe, if only we can keep his injunctions and live a healthy life-style, following the principles of good hygiene,good diet and exercise, which most people breach.

It must also be noted that it is essential to be healthy spiritually, if we are to attain physical health. Oftentimes the Bible warns against anxiety, evil desires and vices. All these pollute our heart and create situations of unrest that affect our physical being and health. "A heart at peace gives life to the body, but envy rots the bones" (Proverbs 14:30). "A cheerful heart is good medicine, but a crushed spirit dries up the bones" (Proverbs 17:22). God feels good when we diligently obey him and keep his precepts. It took God five days to provide all needed materials by man before he made man in his image. He will therefore not bring disaster, hunger or poverty to his image, if we lead a pleasing life. However, through disobedience and refusal to keep his commands, the door was open to all sorts of problems including diseases; and we therefore became susceptible to illness physically. Also due to the activities of some evil ones in the society, man becomes infected with diseases.

The lesson to be learned is that we need to brace up our spiritual health through obedience to God to enjoy physical health; because God had provided us everything needed for us to live a healthy life and he affirmed that all were good (Genesis 1:11, 24–26). Having done that, we should stick to the rules of dieting, environmental hygiene, regular exercise and a good life-style to enjoy good health, because prevention is always better than cure. So it is necessary to eat right, sleep right, do exercise and everything necessary to stay healthy. We must also open up whenever we have any health challenge; realizing the fact that what you know cannot kill you. It is what you do not know, or that you know but hide, that can kill.

(III) THE CELL

The cell is the basic structural, functional and biological unit of all known living organisms. A cell is the smallest unit of life that can replicate itself independently and cells are often referred to as "the building blocks of life". The body has about 60 million cells, all of which have one million pages of information inside the cell DNA. Each of them performs individually unique functions to work up the body system. So, we have bone cells, muscle cells, blood cells, skin cells, heart cells etc.

DNA (deoxyribonucleic acid) is a type of acid which is the hereditary material in humans and almost all other organisms. Nearly every cell in a person's body has the same DNA. Most DNA is located in the cell nucleus.

The cells are fed with fruits and vegetables, lipids and sterols, which are the product of whole grain. Lipids and sterols help to repair damaged cells, reproduce new ones and replace weak cells. It stands to reason that a good diet of fruit and vegetables boost our immunity and make our cells healthy. A healthy cell is the basic foundation for good health. Most people diet to die. Suggesting that most of our diets feed only the stomach and neglect the cells. This is detrimental to healthy living and is responsible for most of the chronic diseases in human society. Excessive smoking and alcoholic intake are also dangerous to health.

If cellular membranes are deficient of vital nutrients of lipids and sterols, they become inflexible and unable to perform their functions. Whole grain lipids and sterols allow the cell membrane to become their flexible best, making it easier for nutrients to get in and waste to get out of the body. GOOD NUTRITION BEGINS AT THE CELLULAR LEVEL.

SOME CHRONIC DISEASES AND THEIR PREVENTION

(1) STROKE

Stroke is the second leading cause of death in Nigeria and other developing countries. The Medical dictionary defines stroke as the sudden death of brain cells due to the interruption of blood supply to the brain. Medical experts warn that stroke is largely caused by hypertension, also known as HBP and closely followed by diabetes, high cholesterol and obesity. They explained that many people are unaware they have high blood pressure (HBP) and that the few that are aware do not have it controlled, either due to lack of access to medication or due to the misconceptions about stroke which is largely borne out of ignorance.

CAUSES

1. Life-style and diet. Some people eat to die rather than eat to diet.
2. Excess intake of carbohydrates, the end result of which is sugar.
3. Eating at odd hours, especially eating late at night and sleeping before digestion. This may result in accumulation of fat in the body. Once you have diabetes, there is the tendency that you will have HBP. Although sugar is needed for energy, it must not be in excess of the required quantity that the Pancreas can break down to be used by the body system.
4. Failure to do exercise. Exercise at regular intervals is necessary to get the body system moving. It allows the heart to work to its full potential. It improves cholesterol and fat levels. Regular exercise helps to reduce inflammation in the arteries. It results in weight loss and ensures the blood vessels to be elastic. It improves blood flow and blood pressure.

The United States Department of Health and Human Services recommends at least one hour of physical activity each day.

5. Failure to drink enough water everyday. It is recommended that an individual takes at least 10 cups of water each day.
6. Excess intake of alcohol.
7. Excess intake of salt.
8. Excessive indulgence in sexual activity. Unrestricted sexual intercourse can result in stroke; since sex triggers up the rate of blood pressure.

Above all, the heart must be kept healthy to perform its functions effectively. This is because the heart is the hardest working muscle in the body. It beats over 100,000 times and pumps over 9,500 liters of blood through the body each and every day. Without a properly functioning heart, the body is deprived of the oxygen and nutrients it needs for optimal functioning. This is why maintaining cardiovascular health is so important - it affects every other part of our body.

However, despite improvements in medicine and technology, cardiovascular disease continues to be the leading cause of death in the world. While it tends to strike men earlier in their lives, it affects both genders and can be a severe and debilitating condition leading to frequent hospitalisations. The good news is that cardiovascular disease can be prevented through diet and lifestyle changes. Studies continue to support the role of exercise, nutrition and healthy diet in preventing heart disease. Cultivate the habit of taking at least a cup of water before bed. It keeps you free from having heart attacks.

Heart attacks often give impending or warning signs and in many cases no warning at all. Warning signs include chest pain on the left side spreading to the left shoulder, which gets worse during increased activity or exercise. These should be taken seriously when occurred and a specialist cardiologist should be contacted for ECG including exercise ECG.

PREVENTION

1. Manage your HBP.
2. Watch your diet, eat right to avoid bad cholesterol in your body.
3. Avoid smoking, the effect of which narrows the blood vessels such that blood can not pass through the arteries easily.
4. Engage in regular exercise.
5. Avoid excessive alcohol and carry out effective control of sugar levels in your body. Once you are prone to HBP, diabetes will come in and it is the roadmap to every other disease, such as liver problem, kidney failure and cardiac arrest.
6. Minimize your meat intake and eat more fish, snails etc.
7. Take fruits and vegetables and more whole grain food than carbohydrates.
8. Avoid being overweight
9. Take a lot of water, at least ten cups a day.
10. Sleep well (8 hours each day)

(2) DIABETES

Diabetes is a number of diseases that involve hormone insulin problems. This causes the glucose levels in the body to drop. There are three types of diabetes: Type 1, Type 2 and Gestational diabetes. Type 1 diabetes is known as juvenile diabetes or insulin-dependent diabetes. It is erroneously believed that Type 1 diabetes is a childhood disease. Although the majority have Type 2 diabetes, an important minority, about 5% have Type 1 diabetes. Contrary to popular belief, Type 1 diabetes is not a childhood disease. Diabetes occurs at every age in people of every race and of every stage and size. In fact, there are more adults who have Type 1 diabetes than children, although it was previously known as juvenile diabetes. In Type 1 diabetes, the body does not produce insulin. The body breaks down the carbohydrates you eat into blood glucose also called blood sugar which it uses for energy. Insulin is a hormone that the body needs to get glucose from the bloodstream into the cells of the body, with the help of insulin therapy and other treatments. Even young children can learn to manage their condition and live long healthy lives. All you need to do is to balance your insulin doses with the food you eat and the activity you do.

Gestational diabetes only happens during pregnancy and may not occur again after child birth. It typically develops between the 24th and 28th weeks of pregnancy. It is a condition in which a woman without diabetes develops high blood sugar levels during pregnancy.

Type 2 diabetes, once known as adult-onset or non-insulin dependent diabetes is a chronic condition. It is a problem with your body that causes blood glucose (sugar) levels to rise higher than normal. It is a life-long condition that causes a person's blood sugar level to become too high. Type 2 diabetes is a progressive condition in which the body becomes resistant to the normal effects of insulin.

PREVENTION

Prevention of Diabetes is as indicated under Stroke since High Blood Pressure may trigger diabetes. Only to add that the following steps need to be taken for Diabetes control.

1. Frequent check of blood glucose level.
2. Decide to use the staircase more instead of elevation.
3. Take medication at the right time and feel happy all the time.
4. Try to own the disease, knowing that you spend less hours with the doctor (May be 5 hours with the doctor in a whole year).

Owning up with the disease makes one do self monitoring of the blood glucose regularly of which Accu Chek blood glucose meter can help achieve better results.

(3) CANCER

Cancer is a group of diseases involving abnormal cell growth with the potential to invade or spread to other parts of the body. These contrast with benign tumors which do not spread to other parts of the body.

There are more than 100 types of cancer; they include (i) breast cancer, (ii) skin cancer, (iii) tongue cancer, (iv) colon cancer, (v) prostate cancer, (vi) lymphoma cancer (cancer that starts in the white blood cell), (vii) cervical cancer, (viii) throat cancer, (ix) brain cancer....

Treatments may include (i) Chemotherapy (ii) Radiation and/or Surgery.

Symptoms include (i) Fever, (ii) Extreme tiredness (Fatigue or weight loss), (iii) Lumps in the body, (iv) Blood in stool or urine, (v) Non-healing sores, (vi) Swollen glands, (vii) Coughing up blood, (viii) Night sweats, (ix) Pain. The earlier cancer is detected, the more likely it is that treatment will be successful.

We will discuss three major types of cancer - (i) Prostate cancer (ii) Cervical cancer and (iii) Breast cancer.

(D) PROSTATE CANCER

Prostate cancer affects men. The prostate is a small walnut shaped gland under men's reproductive organ (the penis) that produces the seminal fluid that nourishes and transports the sperm in men during sexual intercourse.

Prostate cancer is therefore the development or the growth of a cancer cell in the prostate, the gland in the male reproductive organ.

Most prostate cancers are slow in growing, while some grow relatively quickly, the reason why men may not know immediately that they have prostate cancer. The cancer cell may spread from the prostate to other areas of the body if not checked. It is a situation when abnormal cells develop in the prostate. These abnormal cells can continue to multiply in an uncontrolled way and sometimes spread outside the prostate into nearby or distant parts of the body.

CAUSES

1.   These include our diet, Life-style and age. It is also hereditary.

2. From age 35/40 and above one stands the risk of having prostate cancer.
3. Family history is a factor since it is hereditary.
4. Sedentary lifestyle (sitting down for a long period in a place).
5. Untidy underwear, dirty clothes, too tight clothes around men's reproductive organs.

SYMPTOMS

1. Difficulty in urinating.
2. Blood in semen.
3. Scanty ejaculation.
4. Pain during sexual intercourse at the point of ejaculation.
5. Low sexual urge.
6. Much pain around the pelvis, or the reproductive organ.

PREVENTION

1. Constant checkup.
2. Avoid tight pants. Allow fresh air to enter through your reproductive organs.
3. Avoid too many carbohydrates, the end result is sugar which triggers cancerous cells to grow rapidly.
4. Avoid a sedentary lifestyle as much as possible.
5. Go for Prostate Sensitivity Antigen (PSA) tests regularly.

(B) CERVICAL CANCER

Cervical cancer involves women. It is the cancer that affects the entrance to the uterus (womb). The cervix is the narrow part at the entrance to the womb from the vagina. Cervical cancer develops in a woman's cervix. It is due to the abnormal growth of cells that have the ability to invade the cervix. Cervical cancer can be life-threatening if it goes undetected or untreated. Most cervical cancers are caused by a virus in the cells of the cervix. The primary risk factor for cervical cancer is human papillomavirus (HPV) infection.

SYMPTOMS

Most women do not have any signs or symptoms of a precancer. In many women early signs of cervical cancer are uncommon. It may include vaginal discharge. Symptoms of cervical cancer are not always obvious, and it may not cause any problem at all until it has reached an advanced stage. Women with early cervical cancers and precancers usually have no symptoms.

TREATMENT

Like any cancer disease, treatment for cervical cancer depends on how far the cancer has spread, as cancer treatments are often complex. These include screening at an early stage and which can be treated successfully. The stage of cervical cancer is the most important factor in choosing treatment. Treatment options can include surgery, radiation therapy, chemotherapy, medication.

(C) BREAST CANCER

Breast cancer is caused by uncontrollable growth of abnormal cells in the breast. It is the cancer that develops from breast tissue. Breast cancer survival rates are increasing as screening and treatment improve.

SYMPTOMS

These include a lump in the breast, a rash discharge from the nipple or pain in the nipple of the breast. The most common symptom of breast cancer is a new lump or mass. A painless mass that has cancer.

Breast cancer affects both men and women.

PREVENTION:

Prevention includes

1. avoid tight brazier,
2. don't wear brazier to sleep,
3. don't wear brazier more than eight hours in a day,
4. allow fresh air into your breasts,
5. don't drink bottled water that has been in the car and got heated,
6. reduce the intake of fatty foods, especially fried foods.

TREATMENT

The choices of treatment will depend on the type and stage of the breast cancer, the age and overall health of the victim and the type of cancer organism.

Most women with stages I, II or III breast cancers are treated with surgery, often followed by radiation. In recent years, there has been an explosion of life-saving treatment advances against breast cancer. Treatment usually involves a combination of surgery, chemotherapy and radiotherapy. Breast cancer is treated in several ways. It depends on the kind of breast cancer and how long it has developed. Usually after one has been diagnosed with primary breast cancer, the specialist team will offer treatment options.

ENVIRONMENTAL HYGIENE

Environmental hygiene both at the household and at the community levels is very important to get rid of certain viruses that are responsible for certain diseases. It helps to reduce the transmission of health-care associated infections and keeps us free from unnecessary illness. The need to take practical control measures to improve the basic environmental conditions affecting our human health - maintaining a clean and hygienic living environment cannot be overemphasized. It is key to our successful attainment of maximum achievement, as ailing health cannot lead us to achieve our wealth. The reason we say "Health is Wealth".

CHAPTER 3

STRATEGIC RELATIONSHIP

"Two are better than one, because they have a good return for their labor. If either of them falls down, one can help the other up. But pity anyone who falls and has no one to help them up" (Ecclesiastes 4:9–10). Relationships are key to any interaction.

STRATEGIC RELATIONSHIP CAN be defined as an agreement between two or more entities for the purpose of conducting specified activities or processes, to achieve specific objectives such as product development, distribution or rendering of services. It is an alliance between two or more people or groups of people. It occurs between nations and different ethnic groups all around the globe. A thing common with Alliances is that they are strategic partnerships classified according to objectives and level of formality. It is a form of bond.

Any relationship with another business partner or individual requires you to actively seek out and build a bond with someone. The aim is to collaborate to achieve success in a line of business. The capital cornerstone of our lives is such that wealth creation is impossible single-handedly. No one individual or nation exists on its own without external collaboration. Even internal trade also known as domestic trade, which is buying and selling of goods and services within the confines of a country has assumed expansion that attracts forming of alliances to improve the state of the local economy. It is the success in the internal trade that can boost the national morale at external trade. The features of internal or domestic trade, i.e. movement of goods and services to various locations, within the boundaries of the country, the money economy involved in local currency, traders taking the help of various modes of transport to effect transfer of goods to ultimate customers are so complex and expansive that organized cartels are inevitable. This involves collaborative efforts of individuals and groups in the form of alliances.

When it involves external trade which has to do with trading across the country's border, information about the value and volume of goods traded becomes more complex and requires a more comprehensive and detailed coverage by organized bodies of law enforcement officers. External relationships become more complex and more involved in nature and scope, as international trade and services expands in the form of enterprises.

The wealth of any nation is determined by the extent of her strategic relationship with other nations of the world and this assumes for the reason why the different nations of the world enter into trade agreements with one another; importing and exporting and technologies in varying degrees and affecting each other's lifestyle as far as possible. The wealth of a nation is also tied to the level and advancement of its technology development. This is because all countries of the world use resources and aids to extract more from nature than it would otherwise yield. The aids are aimed at and adopted to the fulfillment of existing needs. Locally available materials are used and processed for consumption or further production. Following the pattern of wealth created elsewhere by industrial means, the desire to consume more is aroused. Population increases and so, more needs to be produced for consumption to be satisfied. But traditional technologies are less suited to meet the rising expectations of the people. The next line of action is to adopt innovation which usually results in adapted technology. The world is advanced through the use of technology and civilization would have been impossible through other means.

The countries in the creative plane with regard to the production of advanced technology stand a better chance to become wealthy on account of exportation of its technology to the less privileged countries. This is better supported by the principle of comparative advantage, which refers to the ability of a person or nation to produce a good or service at a lower opportunity cost. There is no doubt however, that wealth creation relies on technological innovation. The reason why the developed world continues to be richer, while the developing ones continue to languish in poverty. Most of the countries of the developed world are producing countries, while the countries of the developing world are consumers. In any relationship to be effective, values and norms of the society are of utmost importance. It is part of a good strategy to choose wisely. George Washington, Ex-American President, once said "it is better to be alone than in bad company". No one wants to associate or share values with violently-prone groups. The relative peace of a nation will therefore determine the extent of its strategic relationship with other nations.

If a country or society would benefit and share values with others, it is essential to take security seriously. Security is the first structure of social existence. It is analogous to what a cell is to the body. Development of the human soul, spirit and body is tied to the level of security enjoyed by the people. Collaboration with other countries with respect to trade cannot be possible without security, as no investor will invest in an insecure environment. Even within the internal boundary, violence against rules and agreed laws and against the accepted norms of the society results in underdevelopment. Take for instance domestic violence against defenseless children and women. Kidnapping and abduction of school children is now rampant in Nigeria and other violent actions between Fulani herdsmen and farmers resulting in the death of innocent people. This is a breach of peace which is very fundamental to the growth and development of a nation. When farmers are prevented from going to their farms and traders are prevented from trading in a secure atmosphere, the outcome is scarce food products and other items of neccesity that are sold at exorbitant prices. There will be general inflation and scarcity of food and material things needed for good living.

What we are saying is that violence, war, insecurity of any nature is antagonistic to strategic relationships. The reason why many of the nations involved in one strife or another undergo poverty, because they can neither attract good friends nor be at rest to develop socially, economically or politically. The wealth of a nation is attached to the extent to which the nation can perfect its strategic relationship with other progressive nations and the extent of stability of peace.

CHAPTER 4

MONEY (THE SEED OF WEALTH)

MONEY IS NEEDED to create wealth because "money is the answer for everything" (Ecclesiastes 10:19b). The purpose for which everyone works is to earn money. Everyone is money conscious, the reason why one is employed to render services.

Money is earned under four quadrants. The best known of which is as an employee. The first quadrant to earn money is to work for an organization or for an individual and earn a salary. Most salary earners are however not favorably disposed to meet their needs not to think of creating wealth from the earned income. Salaries are always low and a source of ridicule that most salary earners are not satisfied and can hardly make ends meet. However, since the basic thing needed to create wealth is money, no matter how low the salary, a wealth-conscious worker would endeavor to save some of his/ her income to further increase his/her income, either by engaging in retail trading or being self employed in addition to his/her primary employment. Some employees engage themselves, either fully or partly in the second quadrant which is the self employed quadrant to earn income.

It is to be noted however that both quadrants are not self-satisfying. In both, time is money. An employee has traded off his time and at the end of each day becomes tired of doing anything else for himself. On the other hand a self employed individual can not make money when he or she is not at the place of employment. The shortchanging occurs in both time and income earned by both the employee and the self employed, such that dissatisfaction is the order of the day. In any way, the struggle continues for wealth creation adventure.

The problem lies in the fact that both quadrants of an employee and self-employed engaged 95% of the human resources to share the financial resources equivalent to 5%. The bulk of the population in this left side of the quadrants signifies the fact that a larger number of people are in the competitive plane rather than the creative plane of the economy. What this suggests is the poverty of the majority. As it is for the individual, so it is for the nation. The developed nations of the world have a larger number of their population in the creative plane and so are much richer than those of the developing world, that are consuming nations.

What do we do to improve our economic condition? As discussed under chapter four; we must develop a partnership relationship that can enhance our earnings. Knowing too well that no individual has sufficient experience, education or ability to ensure the accumulation of great success. You must endeavor to join a "MasterMind" group, such that it is always available in Partnership. This leads to discussion of the individuals at the right hand side of the Income Quadrants - The Business System Owner and the Investor.

It is a fact that at the left side harboring the employees and the self-employed, a larger number of the population were involved but the financial gains are ridiculously low. At the BSO and the Investor quadrant, very few people, just about 5% of the population, are sharing 95% of the Income. But it is also a fact that much more resources need to be amassed to fall into this quadrant.

Gradual saving habits and self discipline can launch one into the BSO and Investor quadrant, through organized planning and alliance with progressive mastermind groups. One has to ally himself with the plans of the mastermind group and work in consonance with the agreement in the effort to accumulate wealth.

There are two types of Business Owners, one without a system and the other with a system. A business owner without a system is a little better than a self employed. A business system owner is an entreprenuer. He has the capacity to make the system running and does not necessarily need to be present in the business to make money. With a business system owner, income increases in a geometric proportion because it comes from various ways. A business system owner organizes his business theoretically and practically using methods. An application of rules and regulations controlling the operation of the business. A system is a broad principle or rules from which specific methods or procedures may be derived. With this system of doing business, the way of progress is opened and everyone involved in the business operations are guided by the principle and standard of performance. More wealth is generated through this quadrant to become an Investor.

The last quadrant of the income earning group is that of an investor. The BSO having acquired fortunes has no option than to invest his money for more wealth to be generated. This launches one into being in the creative plane as business ideas continue to grow as wealth increases. We have very few of these entrepreneurs in the nation but there is no doubt that the more of them appear in the enterpreneurial world the better for the nation or the individuals.

One thing is clear, our desire to be rich must be translated to action by fixing it in our mind. Imagine what to do to be rich. Create a mindset of a rich man through this imagination and desire and create a definite action plan for carrying out your desire. Then begin at once to implement. As you acquire money gradually, try to make good and progressive use of it to acquire your goal of being a wealthy individual. This will determine your choice of an income quadrant. Some people with low entrepreneurial mindset perpetually remain at the employee quadrant, while those entrepreneurial minded graduate through the quadrants to become an investor of repute. It all depends on your mindset. Also it must be noted that it is possible to earn income on the four quadrants at the same time. Some captains of industries pay themselves from the proceeds of their investments.

The importance of all the quadrants in the economic development of a nation must also be emphasized. That one belongs to the employee quadrant does not make one of less importance. Captains of industries and large corporations demand qualified and well-trained professionals. All you must ensure is that you explore every possible means in your profession to reach the peak. Whatever you are, be a good one. It must however be noted that the dynamic nature of the economy and the fact that sole income is never enough, calls for improvements in income earning power, to be able to create value, project it and market it. This idea brings greater fortunes that can keep an individual above poverty and make one live a happier and more satisfactory life. It will also give someone the ability to look for better money-making opportunities and to decide on the fastest way to accumulate wealth. There are many ways of wealth generation open to an enterprising mind but it depends on the person's desire, action plan and commitment. All we are saying is that one's eyes must be opened to opportunities that must be effectively utilized to generate wealth.

Above all, you must believe in yourself that you can achieve greater heights. With this faith and hard work coupled with determination to succeed, wealth is achievable but one must not give up easily while struggling. Suggesting that you must be stubborn in your aggression. Whatever may happen, be yourself. Every situation in life brings out the confidence level which suggests that to be a successful and a wealthy person, you must be brave and courageous to confront your fear and overcome it.

CHAPTER 5

MATERIAL POSSESSION

WITH MONEY MAN possesses other material and property needed to enjoy life and create more wealth. Man acquires property and engages himself in investments. Material possession can either be an asset or a liability. In a bid to create wealth, one has to choose between possessing material for liability or assets. Goods or property may be acquired for the purpose of selling them to generate more wealth in future. These are assets. On the other hand goods are possessed as luxuries which are liabilities.

Merchandising is a sure way of dealing in goods and commodities for sale. When money is acquired it is good business to generate more income through distributive trade and service industries. This accounts for a substantial proportion of economic activities in every nation, whereby wealth is created. Distributive trade is a channel by which goods are being moved from the places of production to the various buyers located across the country.

While some people buy goods that bring them liability, such as luxuries upon which they will be expending money, some buy asset goods that they can sell to earn more income and become wealthy in the process. A good advice is for one aspiring for wealth to spend his money acquiring materials that will make for acquisition of more money. Asset goods. Buy materials you can offer for sale for a profit, or offer services that can attract you more income. Think materially but do not let the love of money overwhelm you. The multiplier effect of money can only be derived when you engage yourself in trading in wares or rendering of services.

Note that you can not be wealthy if all your earned income is used up on liabilities. The reason why you must create an incentive for saving to start up a business with your accumulated capital. All these must be a product of your mindset which will trigger a desire in you to do something new. This desire will be transmitted to action. Wealth can also be generated through recycling of waste products and mining of natural resources. The problem is that if illegal mining of natural resources is not curtailed and the mines safeguarded, the nation's wealth will go into the wrong hands. Monopoly of trade and production is an evil that must be avoided if a nation's wealth will not be skewed. A situation where only one man has the monopoly of trade or to produce and distribute products is an abuse of a free market enterprise. The result usually is undue scarcity in production and an uncontrolled increase in the prices of the affected products, and which will also adversely affect the supply, demand and prices of other products. Poverty thrives in this situation.

Marketing material things calls for certain things which a speculator in material buying and selling must do:

1. *Understand the features of the market.* Acquire knowledge of the market situation, Make an in depth study of the market for the commodities, he has the mind of trading in. The traditional nature of the economy and evaluation of the market situation, present and future, to determine the ease with which the business can be executed.

2. *Evaluation of Customers Needs and Wants.* Marketing is the process of fulfilling the needs of the customers. There is dissimilarity between needs and wants which the traders or suppliers must be able to understand. Needs have to do with what you can not do without while wants have to do with what you desire but which

are not of primary need. You can do without wants, you can not do without needs. Some of the needs of any society include food, shelter, clothing materials and health. Identifying these will make a speculator's involvement in a worthy trade possible.

3. *Satisfaction of Customers.* Much as it is good to have an entrepreneurial mindset and do business to create wealth, entrepreneurial activity is about creating enabling environments for the market to thrive and these include satisfaction of the customers. A focus on full commitment to satisfy customers will include anticipating the needs of the customers and endeavoring to meet them. Absolute integrity in rendering good service and respect for the individual, stand one out as an efficient and effective business owner. Since the multiplier effect of business must be to create a meaningful and satisfying life in the best way possible for the masses, an attempt to create wealth must not opt for negative dealings. The ultimate purpose of our dealings in all spheres must ensure that the output of our performances satisfy the mass of the people, whom we should also respect.

4. *Shun the Dimensions of Poverty.*
    i.   Stop crying and complaining, Be diligent at doing something Be a solution provider and value creator. If you provide solutions to people's problems, they will respect, honor and reward your action.
    ii.   Refuse to live a life of disappointment.
    iii. Don't be ignorant of what rightfully belongs to you. Pursue it.
    iv.   Don't be ignorant of what you have - your potential that can be turned into wealth.
    v.   Don't be lazy, because "lazy hands make for poverty, but diligent hands bring wealth (Proverbs 10:4)
    vi.   Don't be ignorant of what you can do to change your financial situation. Be enterprising and forward looking.
    vii. Don't shun the company of good people. Join the partnership of good and enterprising people. Be identified with the right people and follow them diligently and intelligently. Be progressive in your thinking.

CHAPTER 6

LIFE EXPERIENCE

EXPERIENCE, THEY SAY, is the best teacher. The wealth of your experience matters in your decision to start up a business that can enable you to be wealthy. Much as you can gain experience through involvement in an activity i.e. by working, you can also gain experience through discovery. Experience can also come through ideas. One thing that must be understood about life experience is its dynamic nature. It is never static. It is derived from everyday life occurrences. Each day's experience in life differs from man to man but it is a product of definite desires backed by definite plans, through consistent persistence and perseverance to succeed. Many great inventors and scientists have been launched to fame through their discoveries. The writer of a book discovered that the reason why his book did not sell was not the content but the title of the book. He changed the title of the book and his sales volume increased considerably. There is no end to gaining experience in life which can also be derived from experiments.

A man who worked to retirement age in an employment, must have spent nothing less than 35 years to reach the retirement age and must have attained the age of 60 years. Such a person decided to stay in the employment through thick and thin. In the business circle as well as in employment, persistence, perseverance and determined effort to succeed are qualities that add to the experience of one who stays rather than quit the endeavor. It stands to reason that without persistence, perseverance and determination to achieve, there can be no experience that is much required for a successful achievement. To develop persistence which leads to perseverance and determination in life, the following simple steps become inevitable:

1. A definite purpose by burning desire for its fulfillment. A man of purpose and action is a man who has a dream for the future.

2. A definite plan, experienced in continuous action. Write down your plan in a clear and unambiguous manner and work toward achieving the plan. Assess your achievement through a continuous improvement index of planning, checking whether the plan works, correct any error or abandon the plan for a new one. This is known as the Plan, Do, Check and Act process. The famous PDCA i.e. Plan, Do, Check and Act is a never-ending cycle of improvement strategy which can be applied to all facets of business. To expatiate further, your plan must be executed and the result must be evaluated to see whether the outcome is the expected result. If not, you need to change the plan by substitution and continue the process of assessment. Brace up your ability to build capacity.

3. A mind closed tightly against all negative and discouraging influences, including negative suggestions of relatives, friends and acquaintances. Which means you should avoid discouraging partners. You must be dogged in your determination to attain your desired purpose and be focused on the same.

4. A friendly alliance with one or more persons who will encourage you to follow through with both plan and purpose. Have a mentor but not a tormentor. The mentor must be concerned in offering encouraging words and be passionate to go along with your desire to succeed. Besides, he or she must be sympathetic and identify with your problems.

5. Identification with progressive elements. The company or friends you identify with matters in your effort to acquire wealth. Drunkards and adulterers will always be reckless with

their money rather than saving it. "Whoever walks with the wise becomes wise, but the companion of fools will suffer harm". "Whoever loves pleasure will be a poor man; he who loves wine and oil will not be rich" (Proverbs 13:20, 21:17).

These five steps are essential for success in all walks of life and should form part of the life experience and habit of anyone hungry for success. It is a simple way by which anyone can control his or her economic destiny.

No one in life can leave his/her economic destiny to indecision or to another man's decision and still expect to accumulate wealth. It is high time for one to take a definite decision and plan of action that will bring financial freedom, which is basic to wealth accumulation.

Without a determined effort to take the risk, wealth creation may not be possible. So be a risk taker but it must be calculated risks.

CHAPTER 7

KNOWLEDGE AND SKILLS

KNOWLEDGE IS POWER. The basis of knowledge is information which is also of utmost importance toward achieving success. First of all one should decide the sort of specialized knowledge one requires and the purpose for which it is needed. We often ask our children what they want to become? That is a way of creating in them, the awareness that they exist for a purpose and that their destiny is in their hands. To a large extent your major purpose in life, the goal toward which you are working, will help determine what knowledge you need to pursue. With this question settled, the next move requires that you have accurate information concerning dependable sources of knowledge. The more important of these are:

1. Your own experience and education. Someone with basic education in Arts, cannot hope to become a medical scientist unless of course, he or she changes direction and gets trained in science.
2. Experience and education available through cooperation of others (Mastermind Alliance), partnership, guild societies etc.
3. Colleges and universities available.
4. Public libraries (through books and periodicals in which may be found all the knowledge organized by civilization).
5. Special training courses (through night schools, vocational studies, home studies and correspondence training).

Once acquired, knowledge must be organized and put into use to achieve the definite purpose through practical plans. It must be noted that knowledge has no value except that which can be gained from its application toward some worthy end. You need not take on any course of study until you determine the purpose for which you want the knowledge you are seeking. You can then find out where the particular sort of knowledge can be obtained, from a reliable source.

Success in life is a product of a rich knowledge acquired not only in schools but throughout life endeavors. As you undertake businesses, professions, employment opportunities and other endeavors, you continue to learn. Successful men, in all callings, never stop acquiring specialized knowledge related to their major purpose, business or profession. It is a mistake and a sign of failure of thought to believe that the knowledge-acquiring period ends when one finishes school. The truth is that the school does but little more than put one in the way of learning how to acquire practical knowledge. A specialized man is one who continues to be trained after his acquisition of the school knowledge. It is for this reason that in all endeavors, specialists are most sought and are more successful in whatever they lay their hands on. This is an art of professionalism which is relevant in all endeavors.

It is the art of specialization that brings out your skills and makes you become aware of the need to feel more confident in developing them to make you become a career person. Skills incorporate your experience, bring out your strength, abilities and other qualities that make you a rare gem in the professional world. Skills are the expertise or talent needed in order to do a job or task. It is your skills that make your life and no one intending to achieve success at a job will stop at the point of school education. You can develop your skills through various outlets opened for the acquisition of specialized training i.e. vocational centers.

There is no doubt that the extent to which you are knowledgeable and the wealth of information at your disposal will determine your involvement in activities that will launch you into wealth creation because an educated mind is an enlightened mind. Education opens your imaginative faculty of the mind and widens your ideas for creativity which is also a step toward wealth creation. People believe that "ideas rule the world". You must therefore struggle to acquire educational and professional qualifications or learn skills for gainful employment.

CHAPTER 8

SUMMARY AND CONCLUSION

WEALTH CREATION BEGINS in the form of desire which is the first lap of the journey from the abstract to the concrete, into the workshop of the imagination where plans for its transition are created and organized. In other words, one must have a burning desire to be rich. The mind works on this imagination and transforms it to a plan of action. Wealth creation in concrete terms therefore, is a practical step at doing something that makes you wealthy.

Broadly speaking, there are two types of people in the world - the leaders and the followers. Among these also are two types, the rich and the poor. One has to decide at the outset whether one intends to become a leader or follower in a chosen calling or to become rich or poor as well. This decision is necessary and personal to embark on the startimg point of activities toward achieving goals. It is not a disgrace to be a follower or be poor but there is no credit in remaining a follower or being poor perpetually without a trial to be rich. It must be noted that when we were created we were not leaders but through socialization and internalizations, and toward developing our potential toward achieving the capacity, we become leaders.

Actually, the starting point of most great leaders is to be a follower. They became great leaders because they were intelligent followers. A man who can not follow a leader intelligently can not become an efficient leader. Leadership is learnt at the followership level.

In like manner wealth requires that a man intending to be rich develop the capability to follow the principles of doing things in certain ways which those who are rich actually followed and became successful. They, also, must follow intelligently. Aspiration for acquisition of something, in this wise wealth, is of utmost importance. Practical steps must be taken to aspire for wealth by transferring your desire to the imagination faculty and then taking concrete action to implement it. Believe in yourself that you are capable of being wealthy, through the principle of PBR - Pray, Believe and Receive which is your FAITH. Because Faith itself is the substance of things hoped for - Wealth and evidence of things not seen - Believing that you have Received it, But note that Faith by itself if it is not accompanied by Action is dead. So you demonstrate your desire to be a wealthy man by taking the necessary action aimed at achieving that end. Plan your future. If you plan your future, you will work less in old age. Your plans at achieving your purpose must be detailed and actionable.

Develop a creative mind and not a competitive one. Creativity is an open-door to a wide range of opportunities which are a determinant factor to achieving wealth. Have a positive mindset which is the first step to taking action to fulfill one's purpose in life. Give no room to negative thought or desire for failure. Your desire for success must be greater than your fear of failure. You must have the intention to make good use of any opportunity or advantage that comes your way. Be sure you engage yourself in an undertaking of major importance to you. This suggests that you must show passion for your undertaking and not for the fun of it. Advance your aptitude and career and improve your health.

You may build a place or palace, remember you need people to fulfill your purpose in life and make your dream come through. So, be merciful and show love to all people. Develop the ability to adjust with others. Seek peace with all people. A future awaits those who seek peace. Basically, man is a social animal and no one can survive living alone. Charles Darwin says "It is not the strongest of the species that survive, nor the most intelligent, but those most responsive to change. We must be adjustable and adaptable to survive in all circumstances before we can be a success.

You must be persistent, persevering and determined to achieve your purpose of becoming wealthy and follow the action plan doggedly without allowing any discouragement either from known or unknown people. Be focused and hold on to your faith that your desire will come through. With a strong but flexible mind to succeed, if the first plan you adopt does not work successfully, replace it with a new plan. You may keep on changing your goals as you achieve them, but remain focused that your major achievement is to be wealthy. The point at which the majority of men meet with failure is lack of persistence in creating new plans to replace those which fail. Make no such mistake. The most intelligent man living cannot succeed in accumulating wealth, nor succeed in any other under-taking without plans which are practical and workable. This is a sure and intelligent way of thinking positively and rationally. Be part of this rational thinking. You must also shun laziness, since no lazy man can achieve success. Success is the last of everything. It is not on the surface, yet it is the sweetest of every life event. The need to be successful in any life endeavor is the purpose for which God created us in his image. God sent us to the world empty handed but with certain inborn traits that develop along with us as we grow up and socialize.

God worked hard to create heaven and earth and everything therein, and he will not overlook it if any one is lazy. William James said "In any project the important factor is your belief." Without belief, there can be no successful outcome. You need to think positively and be optimistic to do better. Your driving desires matter in your way to success and laziness must not be a hindrance. Belief in yourself and be confident that you can succeed. Give no room for fear but confront your fear with all your rigor. Remember a lazy man is a failure in life. Do not cultivate his habit.

In all circumstances, acknowledge the providential nature of God as the creator of all things and who also provided these according to His plan. Note that God's time is always the best and work toward the tide and not against it. An attempt to put God aside, and still hoping to appropriate from his providence is one in futility. Have faith in God but believe in yourself. Do not be an atheist or an agnostic whom the Bible regards as a fool. Their knowledge is a negative one, the equivalent of that which Apostle Paul warned Timothy against. "Timothy, guard what has been entrusted to your care. Turn away from godless charter and the opposing ideas of what is falsely called knowledge, which some have professed and in so doing have departed from the faith" (1st Timothy 6:20). Learn wisdom so that you can be favored on your way to achieving your wealth. Anything contrary will lead you to pride which is a step to destruction.

Aspire to live a healthy life both spiritually and physically so that your ability to work toward acquiring your wealth will not be impaired. Guard your heart for everything you do flow from it.

Maintaining cardiovascular health is therefore of utmost importance to ensuring the sustenance of a healthy physique. Ensure you live in a generally disease-free environment through the maintenance of environmental hygiene, knowing that your health determines your wealth. Eat a balanced diet, maintain an acceptable life-style and do exercise at regular intervals. You need to relax, refresh and relate well with people while awaiting your wealth. You must exhibit your lifestyle to avoid ill-health by being guided by these principles.

1. Overeating of food is not conducive to health. Do not be gluttonous.
2. Wrong habits of thought; giving expression to negatives.
3. Wrong use of, and over-indulgence in sex endangers health.
4. Lack of proper physical exercise endangers health.
5. An inadequate supply of fresh air, due to improper breathing endangers health.

6.   Not drinking enough water endangers health.
7.   Find time to rest. Do not develop a 'Superman Syndrome'.

A generally unfavorable environmental infection can trigger illness and shorten one's life.

Maintenance of good strategic relationships is an essential factor to accumulate wealth. Once you determine your purpose, you must think of ways by which the purpose becomes a reality. Be conscious of the fact that you can not do it alone. A good way of raising capital for a business is through equity. Invite trusted parties to share the start-up cost, risks and profits. Since your wealth may be hiding under the very thing you are afraid to do, you need to take a lot of calculated risks. Do not be afraid of anything, but be of good courage to take action based on your major aim, with confidence for success, staying away from negative thoughts and people as much as you can. Remember Fear is 'False evidence appearing real'. You must face and overcome it. The cave you fear to enter may hold the treasure you seek.

You require money and material possessions to further acquire wealth. Many great Business System Owners and Investors borrowed their start-up capital. You should not be afraid to borrow capital for business, provided you have an actionable plan, so that you do not end up being bankrupt if the capital is not put to right use.

Think more of the way to acquire assets rather than liabilities and be self disciplined to ensure frugality. It is true that Business System Owners spend their money on assets and this increases their capabilities to acquire more wealth. Every intending person to acquire wealth must be self-controlled and determined to delay their gratification for luxuries and embrace attitudes that will increase their assets.

Life experience, knowledge and skills are two sides of the same coin which are paramount to achieving wealth. These are factors that hold one up to success in life. Through the help of life experience, acquired education and skills, one is able to move on. Even in a situation of misfortune or temporary defeat. These are the strong backbones of any aspiring man to successful attainments. We often envy men who have accumulated great fortunes, but we do not recognize their way of triumph, we overlook any defeat or misfortune which they had to surmount before their arrival. Anyway, the men would actually have been helped to the extent that they are experienced, persevered, educated and skillful. Application of these attributes engenders strength that propels man to be focused to achieve the goal.

Above all, build your business on honesty and integrity. Be considerate with others in your business, knowing that no wealth or position can endure unless built upon truth, equity and justice. Therefore, you should engage in no transactions which do not benefit all whom it affects. Try to eliminate hatred, envy, jealousy, selfishness and cynicism in all your relationships and transactions and ensure interactions with people on the basis of equity and love for humanity. Remember the injunction that says "Like a partridge that hatches eggs it did not lay are those who gain riches by unjust means. When their lives are half gone, their riches will desert them, and in the end they will prove to be fools" (Jeremiah 17:11).

THE BEAUTY OF WEALTH

"The poor are shunted even by their neighbors, but the rich have many friends" (Proverbs 14:20). Wealth attracts many friends and as the Book of Proverbs rightly says "The wealth of the wise is their crown…"(Proverbs 14:24). When you are wealthy, the assurance is there that you will be able to afford good health and a good diet and live a comfortable life.

Health care is costly and unaffordable by many people. Many people that die prematurely, would probably have been saved if they were able to obtain proper health care.

To a certain extent, wealth gladdens the heart and "A happy heart makes the face cheerful but heartache crushes the spirit" (Proverbs 15:13). Poverty at times causes malnutrition and most of the poor nations of the world find it difficult to feed their population, especially children. So it is good that a nation as well as the individual is wealthy to be able to afford better life for their people.

The wealth of a nation determines her status and the array of her friends on the comity of nations. In actual fact, wealth is an index of a nation's national and international identity. The more wealthy friends you are able to attract, the greater your wealth because wealth has a multiplier effect.

It is to one's honor to aspire to be wealthy, because "money is a shelter" (Ecclesiastes 7:12a) and "is the answer for everything" (Ecclesiastes 10:19b); "A person's riches may ransom their life, but the poor can not respond to threatening rebukes' (Proverbs 13:8). But it is good to follow the right principles to acquire money because "The blessing of the LORD brings wealth, without painful toil for it" (Proverbs 10:22).

Wealth does little or no harm, but can become a snare only to a wicked stingy person. Wealth, if used appropriately, can become a legacy to the generations yet unborn of the wealthy. We often hear about foundations instituted by rich people and the various scholarship awards given by them. All these are made possible through kind-hearted individuals, many of whom have died but left behind their legacies and made their riches to endure.

THE TEMPTATION IN WEALTH ATTEMPT

Our passion for wealth must be controlled so that the love for it will not become a snare and harmful attempt. Wealth can become an idol if care is not taken. In fact, wealth is a deceitful self idol. Don't put your trust on your wealth, so that you will not distance yourself from God and rely on the idol of Mamon. The statement that Jesus made that it would be difficult for those who have wealth to enter the kingdom of God, (Mark 10:25) is to warn us of the snares of putting our trust in wealth. It is much better to live to make others happy with our wealth. Do not live for yourself. Pursuing the love of others through our wealth is a way to demonstrate our love for God (Proverbs 14:31, 19:17, 21:13). Anyone whose love is in money or wealth will be self conceited but yet not satisfied. "He who loves money will not be satisfied with money nor he who loves wealth with his income; this also is vanity" (Ecclessiastes 5:10).

WHAT WEALTH IS NOT

1. Wealth is not the first priority (Matthew 6:33)
2. Wealth is not dishonest gain (Proverbs 28:3). Dishonest gain is a curse (Jeremiah 17:11).
3. Wealth is not for those who dodge pains and seek pleasure (Proverbs 28:19).
4. Wealth is not for a dull, careless and lazy mind (Proverbs 22:29).
5. Wealth is not for those who are blind to see opportunities or close their minds to knowledge (Proverbs 24:5).
6. Wealth is not for a stingy man, who is not ready to affect others positively with his wealth (Proverbs. 11:14, 25–26, 28:8, 22). Because eventually, our body will grow old, and our possessions will fade away. What becomes of value is the impact we have left on others.

THE POSITIVE IMPACT OF WEALTH

As discussed above, the positive impact of wealth can not be overemphasized. It is however a sacrifice of time and energy and most times sleepless nights. However the creative nature of man, also created in the image of God bestows on him wisdom, which if positively employed will launch him to the realization of wealth, which will enable him to fill his house with precious goods. "The LORD by wisdom founded the earth; by understanding he established the heavens; by his knowledge the deeps broke open, and the clouds drop down the dew" (Proverbs 3:19–20). By the same wisdom, knowledge and understanding, a man can acquire his God-given wealth under the sun without regret.

REFERENCES

Kehinde, S.O. (2013) Organizational Behaviour, Processes and Professional Ethics, Fakunsinyayi Commercial Enterprises, Lagos, Nigeria.

Kehinde, S.O. (2018) Understanding The Secrets of God's Blessings (Principles for Prosperity),

SACOM Nigeria Enterprises, Lagos, Nigeria.

Napoleon Hill (2009 Ed.) Think and Grow Rich, Glorious People Bookshop, Lagos, Nigeria.

The Holy Bible

Wealth has an acronym

W -------- What
E -------- Everyone
A -------- Aspire
L -------- Lovingly
T -------- To
H -------- Have

But much as it is important and indispensable, wealth is not a priority or the principal thing. "But seek first his kingdom and his righteousness, and all these things will be given to you as well" (Matthew 6:33). Wealth is part of "all these things" that will be given to the aspirant. The Book is an exposition of the Principles for acquiring wealth. God is the source of true wealth and once this truth is acknowledged, he opens the human mind and strengthens his hands by giving the wisdom and stamina to follow the Principles. "And now Israel what does the LORD your God ask of you but to fear the LORD your God, to walk in obedience to him, to love him, to serve the LORD your God with all your heart and with all your souls and to observe the LORD's commands and decrees that I'm giving you today for your own good?

To the LORD your God belongs the heavens, even the highest heavens, the earth and everything in it" (Deuteronomy 10:12–14 NIV).

It takes the blessings of God to become wealthy. You are advised to read this Book with an open mind to understand the Principles. Note also that striving and struggling precede success and the reason why many people fail is because they think success is an easy task and so they leave what should be done undone. Although hard work is the road to success, the principal thing is to get wisdom, which is the fear of God and the knowledge of the holy One. With this understanding, then you will be able to follow the Principles for wealth creation wisely.

ABOUT THE AUTHOR

S. O. Kehinde is a retired Principal Assistant Registrar at the University of Lagos, Nigeria where he graduated with B.Sc., M.Sc. (Soc.) degrees. He has authored a number of christian and academic books and co-authored some. He is also the author of "Maroko: The Agonies of Displacement" published by Rebonik Publications, Nigeria. Some of his books are Christian books: 1. The Reward of a Faithful Servant, 2. Understanding The Secrets of God's Blessings (Principles for Prosperity), 3. The Challenges of the Lord's Return, 4. Tips for Keeping Christian Homes Together: 55 Wisdom Principles of Enduring Marital Bliss, 5. Understanding Self Idols, 6. Empowered Deacons' Ministry:End-time Blessing to the Church Academic books: 1. Organizational Behaviour, Processes and Professional Ethics, 2. Nigeria's 2007 General Elections in Retrospect: Ethical Issues in Democratic Governance, 3. Theories, Principles and Components of Organizational Behaviour, 4. Communication Networks in Organizational Behaviour. As a Sociologist, S.O. Kehinde's main concern is the establishment of an egalitarian society and eradication of social ills and poverty in the society. Between 2013 and 2020, S.O. Kehinde lectured part time at the Institute of Security, an affiliate of the University of Lagos Nigeria, He is a Baptist Deacon and also a Chaplain of the Chaplains Fellowship of Nigeria Inc.

At the moment, S.O.Kehinde is an overnight maintenance associate at the Walmart, Anna Texas, USA.

S.O. Kehinde is married to Dns. Elizabeth Oyindamola Kehinde and the marriage is blessed to the glory of God.